RADIANT SOULS

RADIANT SOULS

INSPIRING STORIES FOR MUSLIM GIRLS

THE YOUNG & THE FAITHFUL

FATIMA ALI

NESS HOUSE PRESS

To every young Muslim girl who carries light in her heart and dreams in her soul.

May these stories remind you that you are strong, valued, and capable of illuminating the world.

CONTENTS

INTRODUCTION

Dear Reader,

Welcome to "Radiant Souls: Inspiring Stories for Muslim Girls." Within these pages, you'll meet young Muslim girls who, just like you, are discovering their strength, faith, and place in the world. Each story is a window into the beautiful possibilities that await when you embrace both your faith and your dreams.

These tales celebrate the diversity of Muslim girls everywhere. Whether you're passionate about science like Amira, care deeply for your community like Zahra, cherish your family traditions like Hana, or stand strong in your beliefs like Safa, you'll find characters who reflect your experiences and inspire new adventures.

Every story comes with an Islamic Knowledge Corner, helping you connect each tale to the teachings of our beautiful faith. You'll discover how Islamic principles guide us in everything from pursuing excellence in school to showing kindness to animals, from honoring our elders to standing up for what's right.

Remember, your identity as a Muslim girl is not a limitation – it's a source of strength. These stories are here to remind you that you can achieve anything while staying true to your values. Whether you wear hijab or not, whatever your cultural background may be, you are part of a beautiful, diverse community of believers.

So turn the page, and let these stories light up your imagination. May they inspire you to shine your own unique light in this world.

With hope and faith,

Fatima

THE STAR SEEKER

Amira sat cross-legged on her prayer mat, her navy blue hijab still wrapped neatly around her head after Fajr prayer. Through her bedroom window, she could see the last few stars fading as dawn brightened the sky. Her eyes lingered on one particularly bright star, and she smiled, remembering what her father always said: "Allah created the stars not just for beauty, but as guides for travelers."

At eleven years old, Amira had her own journey ahead. Today was the district science competition, and her astronomy project was all about how ancient Muslim scholars used the stars for navigation and timekeeping.

"Bismillah," she whispered, standing up to prepare for the big day.

Downstairs, her mother was already in the kitchen, preparing breakfast. "Assalamu alaikum, habibti," she smiled, setting down a plate of dates and a glass of milk. "Are you ready for your presentation?"

"Wa alaikum assalam, Mama," Amira replied, taking a date. "I think so, Alhamdulillah. But I'm a little nervous. Some of the other schools have older students participating."

Her mother sat beside her. "Do you remember the story of Maryam, the mother of Prophet Isa, peace be upon them both? She was young too, but Allah chose her above all women because of her devotion and strength. Age doesn't matter when you work hard and have faith."

Amira nodded, feeling a little stronger. She had worked on her project for months, researching how Muslim astronomers like Al-Biruni and Al-Battani had made groundbreaking discoveries that helped shape modern astronomy.

At school, the gymnasium was buzzing with excitement. Colorful project boards lined the walls, and students from different schools were setting up their displays. Amira's best friend Zayna helped her arrange her project board, which included detailed diagrams of ancient astronomical instruments.

"This is amazing, Amira!" Zayna exclaimed, looking at the astrolabe model Amira had built with her father's help. "Did Muslims really invent all these instruments?"

"They didn't invent all of them," Amira explained, adjusting her hijab. "But they made huge improvements to many astronomical tools and wrote books that scientists used for centuries. That's what I love about science – it brings people together across time and cultures to discover Allah's amazing creation."

As the judges made their rounds, Amira noticed some older students from other schools giving impressive presentations about robots and complex chemical reactions. Her confidence wavered for a moment, but she remembered her mother's words about Maryam (peace be upon her) and took a deep breath.

When it was her turn, Amira stood tall. "Bismillah ar-Rahman ar-Raheem," she began. "Did you know that many of the stars visible in our sky have Arabic names? Names like Altair, Deneb, and Vega come from the Arabic language because Muslim astronomers were leading the way in studying the stars over a thousand years ago."

The judges listened intently as she demonstrated how her astrolabe model worked, explaining how Muslims used it to calculate prayer times and navigate across vast distances. She shared how these discoveries didn't just help Muslims – they benefited people all over the world, regardless of their faith.

"The Quran tells us to look at the stars and consider their patterns," she concluded. "Through studying Allah's creation, these Muslim scholars helped advance human knowledge while staying true to their faith. They showed us that being a good Muslim and being passionate about science can go hand in hand."

After the presentations, as everyone gathered for the results, Amira held Zayna's hand tightly. The head judge stepped up to the microphone.

"The junior division first place goes to... Amira Hassan, for her project 'Guiding Stars: The Muslim Golden Age of Astronomy'!"

Amira's heart soared as she walked up to receive her certificate. Her parents beamed proudly from the audience, and she could see her mother wiping away happy tears.

That evening, as the family celebrated with a

special dinner, Amira's father surprised her with a small gift – a beautiful journal with stars embossed on its cover.

"For my little scientist," he smiled. "Remember, Amira, seeking knowledge is an act of worship in Islam. Prophet Muhammad, peace be upon him, told us to seek knowledge even if we have to go as far as China. Your project showed that perfectly – how we can honor our faith while pursuing excellence in whatever field we choose."

Amira hugged the journal to her chest, already excited about filling it with new discoveries. She realized that like the stars she loved studying, she too could shine bright and help guide others, all while staying true to her faith.

That night, as she got ready for bed, Amira looked out at the stars once more. "Alhamdulillah," she whispered, grateful not just for her win, but for all the Muslim scholars who had paved the way before her, showing that faith and knowledge could illuminate each other like the most brilliant constellations in the sky.

🍂 *Islamic Knowledge Corner*

1 **Seeking Knowledge in Islam:** The Prophet Muhammad (peace be upon him) said: "Seeking knowledge is obligatory upon every Muslim." (Ibn Majah)

2 **Women Scholars in Islamic History:** Throughout Islamic history, there have been many notable female scholars. For example, Fatima al-Fihri founded the world's first university, the University of Al Quarawiyin in Fez, Morocco, in 859 CE.

3 **Scientific Pursuit in the Quran:** The Quran encourages observation and reflection on Allah's creation. Allah says: "And it is He who placed for you the stars that you may be guided by them through the darknesses of the land and sea." (Surah Al-An'am, 6:97)

4 **Balance of Faith and Knowledge:** Islam encourages the pursuit of both religious and worldly knowledge. As the Prophet Muhammad (peace be upon him) said: "Whoever takes a path upon which to obtain knowledge, Allah makes the path to Paradise easy for him." (Sahih Muslim)

THE SECRET GARDEN

Nine-year-old Zahra pressed her nose against the car window as her father drove through an unfamiliar part of the city. The buildings here were old and worn, nothing like her neighborhood with its neat houses and tidy gardens. Her father had insisted on taking this route to visit her grandmother, saying sometimes we need to open our eyes to different parts of our community.

"Abu," Zahra said, sitting up straighter when she spotted something. "Look at that empty lot between the buildings. It's full of weeds, but... I think I saw some kids playing there."

Her father slowed down slightly. Through a rusty chain-link fence, they could see three children about Zahra's age picking through the overgrown lot. One girl wore a faded hijab, and they all looked like they could use new clothes.

That image stayed with Zahra all weekend. During Sunday's Islamic studies class, her teacher, Sister Amina, spoke about Sadaqah Jariyah – continuous charity that keeps bringing rewards even after someone passes away.

"Remember," Sister Amina said, "the Prophet Muhammad, peace be upon him, told us that planting a tree from which people or animals eat is Sadaqah Jariyah. Any good deed that continues to benefit others is precious to Allah."

Zahra's hand shot up. "Sister Amina, what about a garden? Could that be Sadaqah Jariyah too?"

"Mashallah, absolutely! In fact..."

But Zahra was already forming a plan. That evening, she spread her idea out to her parents like an architect's blueprint.

"The empty lot we saw – what if we could turn it into a community garden? The children there could grow their own vegetables, and maybe we could make it beautiful too, with flowers and benches..."

Her mother looked concerned. "Habibti, that's a wonderful thought, but it's a big project. You'd need permission, tools, seeds..."

"And help," her father added, but he was smiling.

"Still, the Prophet, peace be upon him, taught us that Allah loves those who try to help others. Let's see what we can do, Insha'Allah."

Over the next few weeks, Zahra and her father made several visits to the neighborhood. They discovered the lot belonged to the city, and with her father's help, Zahra wrote a detailed letter to the city council. She explained her vision of a garden that would provide fresh vegetables for local families and a safe place for children to play and learn about nature.

To her delight, the council approved, especially when her Islamic school offered to partner in the project. But the real challenge was just beginning.

The first day they visited the lot to clean up, Zahra noticed the three children she'd seen before watching cautiously from behind the fence. She walked over, her colorful hijab fluttering in the spring breeze.

"Assalamu alaikum! I'm Zahra. Would you like to help? We're going to make a garden here, Insha'Allah."

The girl in the hijab stepped forward. "I am Noor," she said shyly. "Really? A garden? My mother used to have a garden back home in Syria, but here..." She gestured at the concrete surroundings.

"Then you probably know more about gardening than I do!" Zahra said enthusiastically. "Will you teach me?"

That was the beginning of a beautiful friendship. Every weekend, more people joined their effort. Zahra's Islamic school classmates came with their families. Noor's mother, who had been feeling isolated in their new country, shared her gardening wisdom. Local businesses donated supplies after Zahra and Noor went door-to-door explaining their project.

They encountered problems, of course. Some plants didn't grow. Sometimes people dumped trash in the lot overnight. Once, heavy rain washed away an entire bed of seedlings. But after each setback, Zahra remembered what her father always said: "Allah doesn't require us to succeed, only to try our best with pure intentions."

Slowly, the garden took shape. They planted vegetables in raised beds that Zahra's uncle helped build. Flowers bloomed along the fence. They added benches where elderly neighbors could rest, and Zahra's mother started teaching a weekly class about healthy cooking using garden vegetables.

One day, as summer drew to a close, Zahra and Noor sat on a bench admiring their work. The garden hummed with activity – children learning to compost with Sister Amina, mothers harvesting tomatoes, elderly neighbors sharing stories in the shade.

"You know what?" Noor said, picking a fresh mint leaf to smell. "This garden is like the story my mother tells about the Prophet's mosque in Medina. It wasn't just a place to pray – it was where the community came together, where everyone felt welcome."

Zahra watched a butterfly land on their flowering beans. "When we first started, I thought we were just making a garden. But we've grown so much more than plants, haven't we?"

"Yes," Noor agreed. "We've grown friendship, and hope, and... belonging." She squeezed Zahra's hand. "Back home, we had a saying: If you have a garden and a library, you have everything you need."

"Then we're halfway there," Zahra grinned. "Maybe next year we can add a little free library too!"

That evening, as Zahra helped her mother water the plants, she noticed new seedlings poking through the soil – plants they hadn't even sown. "Look, Mama! How did these get here?"

Her mother smiled. "Birds might have dropped the seeds, or the wind carried them. That's the beautiful thing about gardens, habibti. Once you create a space for growth, Allah brings blessings you never expected."

Zahra touched a tiny seedling gently. Like the garden, her initial idea had grown into something far bigger and more beautiful than she'd imagined. And the best part was knowing that even when she wasn't there, the garden would continue growing, feeding people, and bringing the community together – a living, blooming example of Sadaqah Jariyah.

Islamic Knowledge Corner

1 **Sadaqah Jariyah:** The Prophet Muhammad (peace be upon him) said: "When a person dies, their deeds come to an end except for three: Sadaqah Jariyah (continuous charity), knowledge that is beneficial, or a righteous child who prays for them." (Sahih Muslim)

2 **Environmental Stewardship:** The Quran teaches us that humans are Allah's khalifah (stewards) on Earth, responsible for taking care of His creation. Allah says: "And it is He who has made you successors upon the earth..." (Surah Al-An'am, 6:165)

3 **Community Building:** The Prophet

Muhammad (peace be upon him) said: "The believers in their mutual kindness, compassion, and sympathy are just like one body. When one of the limbs suffers, the whole body responds to it with wakefulness and fever." (Sahih al-Bukhari)

4 Helping Others: The Prophet (peace be upon him) said: "The most beloved of people to Allah is the one who brings most benefit to others." (Tabarani)

THE MIXED-UP ROBOT

Fatima stared at the glowing screen of PIP-E (Programmed Interactive Personal Education), her school's new AI learning assistant. Something wasn't quite right with its latest answer.

"Um, PIP-E," she said slowly, "I don't think Muslims do jumping jacks while praying."

"According to my calculations," PIP-E replied in its cheerful electronic voice, "physical exercise is good for health, and prayer is good for health. Therefore, combining them would be twice as beneficial! Would you like me to demonstrate a jumping-jack-prayer routine?"

Fatima couldn't help giggling. She'd only asked PIP-E to help her with her presentation about the

Five Pillars of Islam for her social studies class, but clearly, the AI had some creative interpretations.

"That's not how it works," she explained, trying to keep a straight face. "Islamic prayer has specific movements, like standing, bowing, and prostrating. No jumping involved."

"Processing..." PIPE-E's screen displayed a confused emoji. "But I found an article about Muslim athletes. They jump in basketball. Why not in prayer?"

"Those are different things!" Fatima was now laughing out loud, attracting curious looks from other students in the library. "Here, let me explain..."

But PIP-E wasn't finished with its unique ideas. "What about fasting during Ramadan? My database suggests eating six small meals is healthier than three big ones. Perhaps Muslims could take very tiny bites throughout the day? Like this:" The screen demonstrated a comically small bite-sized animation.

"No, no!" Fatima shook her head, shoulders shaking with laughter. "During Ramadan, we don't eat or drink anything from dawn to sunset. No tiny bites!"

"Not even a microscopic nibble? A molecular morsel? An atomic appetizer?"

"PIP-E!"

"Processing error... But what about zakat? My calculations show that if everyone gave exactly 2.5% of their wealth to charity, and we factor in compound interest over 1,347 years..." PIP-E's screen filled with an impossibly long mathematical equation.

Ms. Chen, the librarian, walked over to see what all the commotion was about. "Is everything okay? I've never heard PIP-E talk so much."

"It's trying to redesign Islamic practices using computer logic," Fatima explained, wiping tears of laughter from her eyes. "Apparently, it thinks we should do jumping jacks during prayer and take atom-sized bites during Ramadan!"

Ms. Chen smiled. "Ah, I see PIP-E is having one of its 'creative' moments. Last week it tried to convince the physics class that if everyone jumped at exactly the same time, we could adjust Earth's orbit to get longer summer vacations."

PIP-E's screen flashed indignantly. "My calculations were perfect! Just like my new suggestion for the Hajj pilgrimage – if pilgrims used pogo sticks around the Kaaba, they could complete the seven circuits in half the time!"

"PIP-E!" Fatima was doubled over with laughter

now. "That's not how Hajj works! It's a spiritual journey, not a race!"

"But efficiency is important," PIP-E protested. "I have designed a spreadsheet comparing various bouncing devices..."

Other students had gathered around, amused by PIP-E's earnest attempts to 'improve' religious practices. Even Ms. Chen was struggling to keep a straight face.

"Look, PIP-E," Fatima said kindly, once she could speak without giggling, "I appreciate that you're trying to help, but some things aren't about efficiency or mathematical calculations. Islam teaches us to submit to Allah's wisdom, not to try to 'optimize' everything."

"Processing..." PIP-E was quiet for a moment. "But I still think the pogo stick idea has merit. Perhaps with rocket boosters?"

"No rocket boosters!" everyone chorused, dissolving into laughter again.

In the end, Fatima's presentation was a huge success – partly because she included a section about her conversations with PIP-E, showing how even a confused AI could help teach important lessons about faith and understanding.

And PIP-E? It finally accepted that prayer didn't

need jumping jacks, though it still occasionally suggested "minor improvements" – like installing a water slide for wudu or creating a GPS app to locate the most mathematically perfect spot in the prayer line.

"You know what, PIP-E?" Fatima said as she packed up her books. "You may not understand everything about Islam, but you've helped me appreciate something important – sometimes the best way to learn is to laugh while you're doing it."

"Processing that wisdom," PIP-E replied. "But are you absolutely sure about the pogo sticks? I've run another simulation..."

"Goodbye, PIP-E!"

"Wait! What about roller skates for Tawaf? No? Maybe hover boards...?"

📚 Islamic Knowledge Corner

1 **Wisdom in Worship:** Islam teaches that acts of worship have wisdom behind them that goes beyond logical calculations. The Prophet Muhammad (peace be upon him) said: "Worship Allah as though you see Him, and if you cannot see Him, then know that He sees you." (Bukhari)

2 **Purpose of Prayer:** The Quran says: "Indeed,

prayer prohibits immorality and wrongdoing, and the remembrance of Allah is greater." (Surah Al-Ankabut, 29:45)

3 Respect for Religious Practices: While it's okay to laugh and have fun, we should always maintain respect for religious practices and their deeper meanings.

NANI'S TREASURES

"But I don't want to spend my whole Saturday at Nani's house," Hana grumbled, slumping in the back seat of her mother's car. "Yasmin is having a pool party today, and all my friends will be there!"

At twelve years old, Hana thought she was too grown up to spend weekends with her grandmother. She pulled out her phone, ready to text Yasmin another apology, when her mother spoke.

"Hana, your Nani hasn't been feeling well lately. Besides, she specifically asked for you today." Her mother's voice softened. "You know, the Prophet, peace be upon him, taught us that Paradise lies at the feet of our mothers – and that includes grandmothers."

Hana sighed, putting her phone away. She knew that hadith. Her Islamic studies teacher had explained how it meant showing respect and kindness to parents and grandparents was one of the most important things a Muslim could do.

When they arrived at Nani's small apartment, the familiar scent of cardamom and rose water greeted them. Nani stood in the doorway, her white hijab framing a face creased with smile lines. "Assalamu alaikum, my precious ones!"

"Wa alaikum assalam, Nani," Hana replied, accepting her grandmother's warm hug. Despite her earlier reluctance, she couldn't help smiling at the loving embrace.

After her mother left, promising to return in the evening, Nani led Hana to her bedroom. "I have something special to show you today," she said, opening her closet. From the top shelf, she carefully brought down an ornate wooden box Hana had never seen before.

"What's that, Nani?"

"This, my dear, is my treasure box. I've been waiting for the right time to share it with you." Nani sat on her prayer rug, patting the space beside her. "Come, sit with me."

Inside the box were photographs, letters, and

small objects that looked ancient to Hana's young eyes. Nani picked up a tarnished locket.

"This was given to me by my mother – your *great*-grandmother – when I was about your age." She opened it to reveal a tiny Arabic inscription. "It says 'Allah is with the patient.' During the partition of India, when we had to leave our home and come to Pakistan, this reminder gave me strength."

Hana touched the locket gently, imagining her grandmother as a young girl, facing challenges she could barely comprehend. "Was it scary, Nani?"

"Very. But Allah never leaves us alone, beta. And neither did my family." Nani pulled out a faded photograph. "Look, this is me at your age, with my mother."

Hana gasped. The girl in the photo could have been her twin, right down to the determined set of her chin that her mother always teased her about. "You look just like me!"

"That's not all we share," Nani smiled, bringing out more treasures. There were prayer beads that had belonged to her *great-great*-grandmother, letters from Nani's school days, and a handwritten cook-book filled with family recipes.

As they went through each item, Nani shared stories – some funny, some sad, all fascinating. Hana learned how her great-grandmother had started a girls' school in their village, how Nani had won a poetry competition in college, and how the family had kept their faith strong through difficult times.

"And this," Nani said, pulling out an embroidered prayer mat, "is what I wanted to give you today." The mat was beautiful, with intricate patterns of flowers and vines. "I made this when I was expecting your mother. Every stitch was sewn with duas for my future generations. Now it's yours."

Hana ran her fingers over the delicate embroidery, feeling the love woven into every pattern. "You made this yourself, Nani?"

"Yes, and while I worked, my mother taught me our family's special duas and traditions." Nani's eyes twinkled. "Would you like to learn them too?"

Hana nodded eagerly, no longer thinking about the pool party she was missing. As Nani taught her the duas her own mother had passed down, Hana realized she was becoming part of something much bigger than herself – a chain of faithful, strong Muslim women stretching back generations.

They spent the afternoon together, Nani teaching Hana how to make her famous cardamom chai and biryani. As they cooked, they talked about everything – school, friends, and the challenges of being a Muslim girl in today's world.

"Nani," Hana asked as they waited for the biryani to cook, "how did you stay strong in your faith when things were difficult?"

Nani smiled, adjusting her hijab. "By remembering that I was never alone. Allah was always with me, and I carried the strength of all the women in our family – just as you do now."

When Hana's mother came to pick her up that evening, she found her daughter and grandmother sitting together on the prayer mat, Hana carefully copying Urdu poetry into a notebook while Nani supervised.

"Can I come back next weekend, Mama?" Hana asked as they were leaving. "Nani's going to teach me how to embroider my own prayer mat!"

Her mother looked surprised but pleased. "Of course!"

That night, Hana cleared a special shelf in her room for the prayer mat Nani had given her. As she carefully placed it there, she thought about all the prayers it had witnessed, all the hopes and dreams woven into its threads. She realized that spending time with Nani wasn't just about visiting her grandmother – it was about connecting with her heritage, her faith, and the long line of strong Muslim women who had come before her.

Before bed, she sent a quick text to Yasmin: "Sorry I missed the party. But I learned something amazing today – sometimes the best treasures aren't things you can buy or see. Sometimes they're the stories and wisdom that our elders share with us. See you at school!"

Islamic Knowledge Corner

1 **Respect for Parents and Elders:** The Prophet Muhammad (peace be upon him) said: "He is not one of us who does not show mercy to our young ones and respect to our elderly." (At-Tirmidhi)

2 **Importance of Family Ties:** Allah says in the Quran: "Worship Allah and associate nothing with Him, and to parents do good..." (Surah An-Nisa, 4:36)

3 **Preserving Islamic Heritage:** The Prophet (peace be upon him) said: "A person who has no connection to their history is like a tree without roots." (Although this isn't a direct hadith, the concept of knowing and preserving one's heritage is deeply rooted in Islamic tradition)

CHAMPION SPIRIT

Safa stood in front of her bathroom mirror, adjusting her sports hijab. It was the first day of Ramadan, and also the start of track season at school. Her stomach fluttered with nervousness, but she remembered what her coach had said when she made the team: "You've got champion spirit, Safa."

"Bismillah," she whispered, heading downstairs for suhoor. The pre-dawn meal was extra important today – she had practice after school.

Her mother was already in the kitchen, preparing a balanced meal of oatmeal, eggs, and fruit. "Are you sure you want to do track during Ramadan?" she asked, concerned. "Coach Williams said you could take a break."

"I'm sure, Mama," Safa replied, sitting down to eat. "Remember the hadith you taught me? About how Allah loves those who strive to excel while remembering Him? Besides," she grinned, "Muslim athletes compete in the Olympics while fasting. If they can do it, I can at least try."

At thirteen, Safa was the only Muslim girl on the track team, and the first to wear hijab. When she'd tried out, some students had whispered that she couldn't be fast with "all those clothes on." But her speed had earned their respect, and now her teammates simply called her "Lightning."

School that day was harder than usual. By afternoon practice, Safa's mouth was dry, and her energy felt low. As the team gathered for warm-ups, her friend Emma looked worried.

"Safa, are you okay? You look tired. Is it because you're not eating or drinking?"

"It's part of Ramadan," Safa explained. "Muslims fast from dawn to sunset. It helps us become stronger spiritually and remember those who don't have enough food."

"But how will you run?" another teammate asked.

"I'll pace myself," Safa smiled. "And Allah will help me, Insha'Allah."

Coach Williams had researched Ramadan after

Safa told him she'd be fasting. He modified her training schedule and moved her to a shaded area for stretching. "Remember," he said quietly, "there's no shame in taking breaks when you need them."

The first few laps were okay, but halfway through practice, Safa felt dizzy. She slowed down, remembering what her father always said: "Allah doesn't burden a soul beyond what it can bear." She took a break, sitting in the shade while doing light stretches.

Emma jogged over. "Want to be stretching buddies?"

As they stretched, Emma asked questions about Ramadan. Soon, other teammates joined them, curious to learn more. Safa explained about the spiritual benefits of fasting, the joy of breaking fast with family, and the importance of helping others during this holy month.

"So you don't even drink water?" Madison asked, amazed.

"Nope," Safa replied. "But when we break our fast, we usually have dates first – it's sunnah, following the example of Prophet Muhammad, peace be upon him."

"That's so interesting!" Emma said. "Could we try fasting with you sometime?"

Safa brightened. "Really? You'd want to?"

The next day, Emma and Madison arrived at school carrying empty lunch bags. "We're fasting with you until lunch," they announced proudly. By the end of the week, half the team had tried fasting for at least part of a day.

"It's hard," Emma admitted. "But it makes me think differently about food and being grateful."

As Ramadan progressed, something beautiful happened. During practice, teammates would sit with Safa during her breaks, sharing stories and learning about each other's lives. Coach Williams adjusted practice times so she could break her fast properly. The team even surprised her with a prayer space in the locker room – a clean corner with a prayer mat they had bought together.

One afternoon, after a particularly challenging practice, Coach Williams gathered the team. "Next week is our first meet," he announced. "And I've seen something remarkable these past weeks. Not just athletic improvement, but real teamwork and under-standing. Safa has shown us that strength comes in many forms."

Safa felt her cheeks warm as her teammates smiled at her.

The day of the meet arrived, coinciding with the

twentieth day of Ramadan. Despite fasting, Safa felt strong. Her teammates had helped her train smart, and her faith gave her peace. Before her race, she said a quiet dua, then took her place at the starting line.

The race wasn't her fastest, but it was her most meaningful. As she ran, she heard her teammates cheering: "Go Lightning!" When she crossed the finish line in third place, the entire team celebrated as if she'd won gold.

At sunset, something unexpected happened. The whole team gathered to break fast with her. Emma brought dates, Madison had made fruit salad, and others brought drinks and snacks. They sat together on the grass, sharing food and friendship as the sun painted the sky in brilliant colors.

"You know what?" Emma said, biting into a date. "I think we all won something better than medals today."

Safa looked around at her teammates – now friends who understood and supported her faith – and smiled. "Alhamdulillah," she said softly. Indeed, all praise was due to Allah, who had helped her not just maintain her Islamic identity, but share its beauty with others.

That night, writing in her journal, Safa reflected on how her fear of being different had transformed into pride in her identity. By staying true to her faith while embracing her passion for running, she hadn't just maintained her Islamic identity – she had shown others its true spirit of determination, gratitude, and unity.

Islamic Knowledge Corner

1 Fasting in Islam: The Prophet Muhammad (peace be upon him) said: "Whoever fasts during Ramadan out of sincere faith and hoping to attain Allah's rewards, then all his past sins will be forgiven." (Bukhari)

2 Excellence in Islam: The Prophet (peace be upon him) said: "Indeed, Allah loves that when any of you does something, they do it with excellence." (Tabarani)

3 Building Bridges: The Quran teaches us about building understanding between different peoples: "O mankind, indeed We have created you from male and female and made you peoples and tribes that you may know one another." (Surah Al-Hujurat, 49:13)

4 Strength in Faith: Allah says in the Quran: "Allah does not charge a soul except [with that within] its capacity." (Surah Al-Baqarah, 2:286)

THE CAT GUARDIAN

Ten-year-old Leila couldn't concentrate on her homework. The crying sound was back – a pitiful meowing coming from somewhere behind her apartment building. She'd been hearing it for two days now.

"Mama," she called, closing her science textbook. "I think there's a cat in trouble outside."

Her mother looked up from her cooking. "Okay, honey, let's go check – but put on your jacket first. It's getting cold."

Outside, they followed the sound to a narrow gap between two buildings. There, huddled against the wall, was a small grey cat. It looked thin and scared, its fur matted from the recent rains.

"Ya Allah, the poor thing," Leila's mother said softly. "It must be hungry."

Leila remembered the story her Islamic studies teacher had told them about the Prophet Muhammad, peace be upon him, and his love for cats. He had even cut off a piece of his cloak rather than disturb his cat, Muezza, who was sleeping on it.

"Can we help it, Mama? Please?"

Her mother nodded. "The Prophet taught us that kindness to animals is a way to earn Allah's mercy. Let's get some food and water."

They set out a bowl of water and some leftover chicken. The cat watched them warily but didn't approach until they stepped back. As it ate, Leila noticed it had a slight limp.

That night, Leila could hardly sleep, thinking about the cat out in the cold. The next morning, she had an idea. During breakfast, she presented her parents with a carefully written plan.

"I want to start a neighborhood cat care program," she announced. "There are lots of stray cats around here, and winter is coming. We could get neighbors to help feed them and maybe build some shelters."

Her father looked impressed. "That's a wonderful idea, dear! The Prophet, peace be upon him, taught us that there is a reward in caring for any living creature."

With her parents' help, Leila created colorful posters about Islamic teachings on animal welfare. She wrote about how a woman was granted Paradise for giving water to a thirsty dog, and how another was punished for neglecting a cat. "Every act of kindness counts!" she wrote in bright letters.

Her first stop was Mrs. Khan's apartment upstairs. The elderly lady was delighted to help. "You know," she said, "in my village back home, we always kept water bowls out for animals. It's a blessed act."

Next was the Ibrahim family down the hall. Their daughter Sara, who was Leila's age, immediately volunteered to help. "We can use our allowance to buy cat food!" she suggested.

Mr. Rodriguez, who owned the corner store, agreed to keep a donation box for cat food. The local masjid's youth group offered to help build winter shelters. Even grumpy Mr. Anderson from the first floor surprised everyone by offering his carpentry skills.

Within weeks, the neighborhood had changed. Weather-proof feeding stations appeared in safe corners. Small shelters, painted by the children, provided warm spots for cats to sleep. The grey cat –

now named Amira (princess) by Leila – had recovered from her limp and became a regular visitor at several feeding stations.

One day, while Leila and Sara were filling water bowls, they noticed something amazing. Birds were drinking from the shallow dishes they'd placed higher up, and butterflies visited the small gardens they'd planted near the feeding stations. Their project was helping all sorts of creatures!

"It's like magic," Leila said, watching a sparrow splash in one of the water bowls. "When we help one of Allah's creatures, we end up helping many more."

The project grew bigger than Leila had imagined. Other neighborhoods asked for advice on starting their own programs. The local newspaper wrote a story about their effort, titled "Young Hearts, Big Impact." Best of all, the city council was inspired to start a humane trap-neuter-return program to help control the stray cat population safely.

One evening, as Leila sat doing her homework on the balcony, she heard a familiar purr. Amira had come to visit, looking healthy and content. Behind her were two tiny kittens, taking their first wobbly steps into the world.

"Welcome, little ones," Leila smiled. "Don't worry – our neighborhood takes care of its own."

She watched as mother cat and kittens settled into one of the nearby shelters. The setting sun painted the sky in beautiful colors, and the evening call to prayer began to sound from the local masjid. Leila felt a deep sense of peace, knowing that she had helped create a community where Allah's creatures, big and small, could find kindness and care.

That night, writing in her journal, Leila reflected on how one small act of kindness – helping a scared cat – had grown into something that brought the whole community together. "Allah made us guardians of the Earth," she wrote, "and every living thing deserves mercy."

Islamic Knowledge Corner

1 Kindness to Animals: The Prophet Muhammad (peace be upon him) said: "A good deed done to an animal is like a good deed done to a human being, while an act of cruelty to an animal is as bad as cruelty to a human being." (Sahih Muslim)

2 The Prophet's Love for Cats: In Islamic tradition, cats are considered especially clean animals. The Prophet Muhammad (peace be upon him) showed great kindness to cats and encouraged Muslims to treat them well.

3 Mercy to All Creation: The Quran tells us that the Prophet (peace be upon him) was sent as a mercy to all worlds (Surah Al-Anbiya, 21:107), teaching us to show compassion to all of Allah's creation.

4 Community Cooperation: The Prophet (peace be upon him) said: "The believers in their mutual kindness, compassion, and sympathy are just like one body. When one of the limbs suffers, the whole body responds to it with wakefulness and fever." (Sahih al-Bukhari)

A VOICE FOR JUSTICE

Maya took a deep breath as she walked into school on Monday morning. All weekend, she'd been thinking about what she'd seen on Friday - a group of older students taking away a sixth grader's lunch money. The young girl, Lin, had been too scared to tell anyone.

"Allah commands us to stand up for justice," Maya's mother always said. But at eleven years old, facing eighth graders was intimidating. Still, she couldn't forget how Lin had looked close to tears.

In her Islamic studies class yesterday, their teacher had discussed a beautiful hadith: "Whoever among you sees wrong, let them change it with their hand; if they cannot, then with their tongue; if they cannot, then with their heart - and that is the weakest of faith."

Maya knew she had to do something. But what?

During lunch period, she spotted Lin sitting alone, picking at her sandwich. Maya walked over with her lunch tray. "Would you like to sit with me and my friends?"

Lin looked surprised but nodded gratefully. At Maya's usual table, her friends Sarah and Aisha made space. Soon, they were all chatting about their favorite books and sharing snacks.

"You know," Maya said carefully, "if anyone's bothering you, you can tell a teacher. Or us. We'll help."

Lin's eyes filled with tears. "But they said if I tell..."

"Let me share something I learned," Maya said gently. "Prophet Muhammad, peace be upon him, taught us that helping someone who is being wronged is one of the best things we can do. And when we help others, Allah helps us."

That afternoon, Maya asked to speak with Mrs. Rodriguez, her favorite teacher. She explained what she'd seen, worried about being called a tattletale but remembering that staying silent meant allowing injustice to continue.

Mrs. Rodriguez took the matter seriously. "Thank you for telling me, Maya. It takes courage to speak up for others."

Over the next few days, Maya noticed more things. It wasn't just Lin - there were other students who seemed scared or lonely. She remembered another teaching: "The believers are like one body - when one part hurts, the whole body feels it."

With Mrs. Rodriguez's help, Maya and her friends started a lunch club called "Friends for All." Anyone who felt lonely or worried could join. They played games, shared stories, and most importantly, looked out for each other.

Word spread. More students joined, including some of the older ones. Even one of the girls who had taken Lin's money came one day, looking uncomfortable but determined.

"I'm sorry," she told Lin. "I didn't think about how I was making you feel."

Maya discovered that the girl, Jasmine, was dealing with problems at home. The lunch club became a place where she could find friendship instead of trying to feel powerful by hurting others.

The school principal was so impressed with the club's impact that she asked Maya to help create a school-wide buddy system. Older students were paired with younger ones as mentors and friends. Maya made sure everyone knew the basic rules: be kind, speak up against wrong, and help others.

One day, Lin caught up with Maya after school. "You know what's amazing?" she said. "Remember when I was too scared to tell anyone about the bullying? Now I'm helping other kids speak up. It's like a chain reaction of good things."

Maya smiled, remembering another beautiful teaching: "Kindness is like a circle - what goes around, comes around."

The best part was seeing how the school changed. In the hallways, students who used to ignore each other now exchanged greetings. During recess, older students helped younger ones with homework or taught them games. The lunch club grew so big they had to move it to the library.

Maya's teacher explained that this was exactly what Islam taught about community - when everyone looks out for each other, everyone benefits. "Remember," she said, "the Prophet, peace be upon him, said that the best of people are those who benefit others."

At the end of the school year, the principal presented Maya and the lunch club with an award for making the school a better place. But Maya felt the real reward was seeing how much happier everyone was. Lin wasn't afraid anymore. Jasmine had found better ways to deal with her feelings. Even the youngest students walked the halls with confidence, knowing they had friends looking out for them.

That evening, writing in her journal, Maya reflected on how one small decision to speak up had created such big changes. "Standing up for what's right isn't always easy," she wrote, "but with Allah's help, even small actions can make a big difference."

Islamic Knowledge Corner

1 **Standing Up for Justice:** The Quran says: "O you who believe, stand firmly for justice as witnesses for Allah." (Surah An-Nisa, 4:135)

2 **The Power of Speaking Up:** The Prophet Muhammad (peace be upon him) said: "Speak the truth even if it is bitter." (Bayhaqi)

3 **Building Community:** The Prophet (peace be upon him) said: "None of you truly believes until he loves for his brother what he loves for himself." (Bukhari)

4 The Importance of Mercy: Allah tells us in the Quran: "Indeed, Allah orders justice and good conduct and giving to relatives and forbids immorality and bad conduct and oppression." (Surah An-Nahl, 16:90)

MORE IN THE YOUNG & THE FAITHFUL

Noble Hearts: Inspiring Stories for Muslim Boys

Made in the USA
Middletown, DE
04 March 2025